Giving Thanks

Sharon Coan, M.S.Ed.

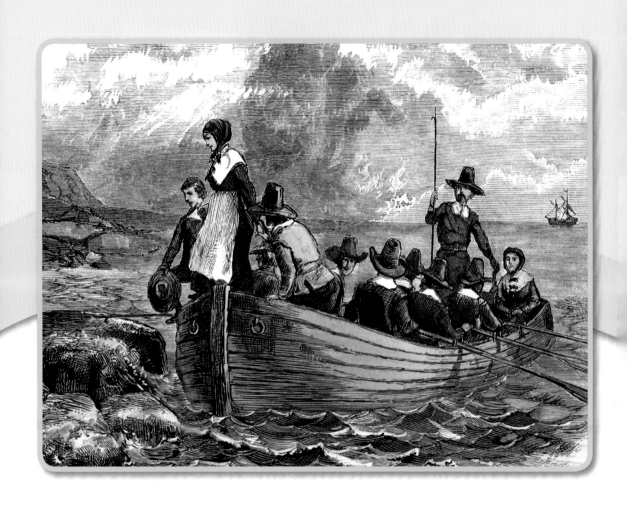

The Pilgrims came
on a ship.

They made friends.

They gave **thanks**.

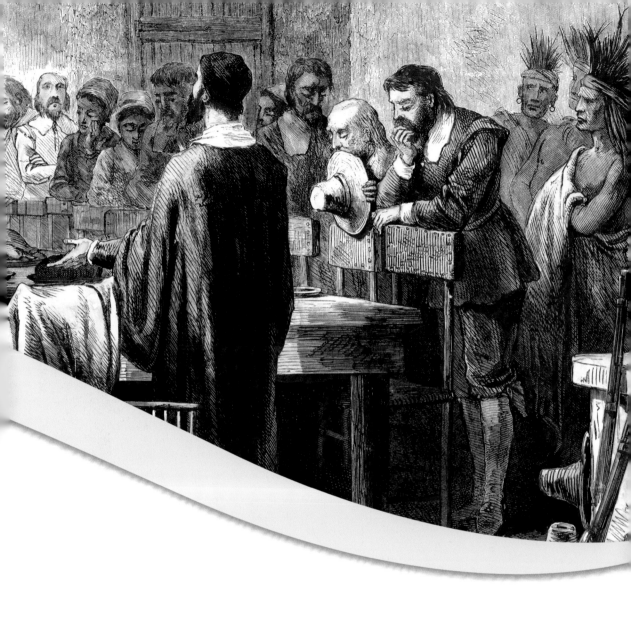

They ate food.

We come in a plane.

We make friends.

We give thanks.

We eat food.

List It!

1. What are you thankful for?

2. Think of three things.

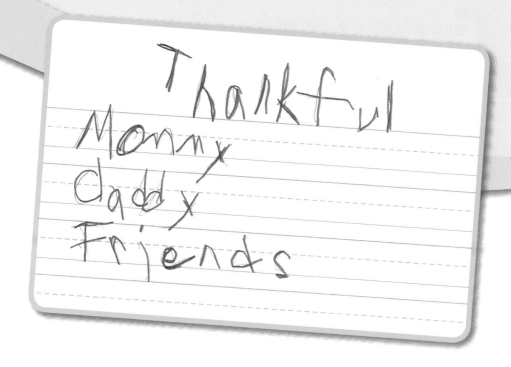

3. Write a list.

Glossary

Pilgrims—the first people who came from England to America

thanks—showing that you are happy and grateful

Index

food, 8, 16

friends, 4, 12

Pilgrims, 2

thanks, 6, 14

Your Turn!

What do you do on Thanksgiving? Draw a picture.

Consultants

Shelley Scudder
Gifted Teacher
Broward County Schools

Caryn Williams, M.S.Ed.
Madison County Schools
Huntsville, AL

Publishing Credits

Conni Medina, M.A.Ed., *Managing Editor*
Lee Aucoin, *Creative Director*
Torrey Maloof, *Editor*
Lexa Hoang, *Designer*
Stephanie Reid, *Photo Editor*
Rachelle Cracchiolo, M.S.Ed., *Publisher*

Image Credits: p.8 ClassicStock/Alamy; pp.11, 23 (top) Blend Images/Alamy; p.12 Design Pics Inc./Alamy; p.3 Bridgeman Art; p.4 Archive Photos/Getty Images; p.17 Sean Justice/Getty Images; p.14 RonTech2000/iStockphoto; p.23 (bottom) fotostorm/iStockphoto; p.15 DNY59/iStockphoto; p.16 monkeybusinessimages/iStockphoto; p.22 Bryngelzon/iStockphoto; p.13 digitalskillet/iStockphoto; p.24 pushlama/iStockphoto; p.6 LOC [LC-H824- P01-057]/The Library of Congress; p.9 LOC [LC-USZC4-4961]/ The Library of Congress; pp.2, 5, 7 North Wind Picture Archives; p.19 Teacher Created Materials; All other images from Shutterstock.

Teacher Created Materials
5301 Oceanus Drive
Huntington Beach, CA 92649-1030
http://www.tcmpub.com
ISBN 978-1-4333-7341-1
© 2014 Teacher Created Materials, Inc.